BAKE IT EASY

GLUTEN-FREE

BREAD MACHINE

COOKBOOK

The ultimate guide to baking tasty

loaves with the use of a bread machine

By

Emily Willem

Table of Contents

INTRODUCTION

Welcome to Baking made easy: The ultimate gluten free Bread Machine Cookbook! Whether you're recently leaving on a gluten free way of life or have been exploring it for a really long time, this cookbook is intended to assist you with excelling at gluten free bread making — rapidly and easily, utilizing your dependable bread machine.

Baking gluten free bread at home can be a unique advantage. Locally acquired gluten free bread frequently misses the mark in surface and flavor, leaving you longing for the glow and newness of handmade portions. With a bread machine, you can appreciate delicate, delectable gluten free bread without the mystery or manual exertion, simplifying the whole interaction and calm.

In this cookbook, you'll find all that you really need to begin: from understanding gluten free fixings to utilizing your bread machine's settings flawlessly. We'll cover fundamental tips and deceives for fruitful gluten free bread making, with recipes that reach from exemplary portions to inventive, exquisite, and sweet varieties. There's something for everybody — whether you're searching for sandwich bread, supper rolls, or specialty choices for paleo and vegetarian diets.

Prepare to open the delight of baking gluten free bread with ease, flavor, and certainty. Your kitchen is going to smell amazing!

Welcome to gluten-free Baking

Gluten-free baking can feel like an uncharted area for some, yet it doesn't need to be. Whether you're gluten-bigoted, have celiac sickness, or are essentially investigating a without gluten-free way of life, you're in the right place! Baking without gluten is accompanied its own remarkable difficulties, yet with the right methods and a touch of tolerance, you can make breads that are similarly as delightful, fluffy, and fulfilling as their gluten-filled partners.

Gluten, the protein tracked down in wheat, rye, and grain, gives customary bread its construction and versatility. At the point when we eliminate it, we need to re-examine how to assemble that equivalent surface with different fixings. However, here's the uplifting news: with the developing accessibility of gluten-free flours and bread machine innovation, baking gluten-free bread at home is more straightforward than at any other time.

This cookbook is intended to be your aid, offering bit by bit guidelines, tips, and secure recipes to assist you with baking your best gluten-free bread. You'll find out about the fundamental fixings that emulate gluten's properties, as xanthan gum and psyllium husk, and how to join different gluten-free flours, like rice, sorghum, and tapioca, to accomplish the ideal surface and taste.

Gluten-free baking is more than just a diet — it's a chance to find new flavors and surfaces. Whether you're heating up for yourself or your friends and family, you'll before long understand that gluten-free doesn't mean without taste. With your bread machine close by, you'll be preparing warm, natively constructed portions effortlessly.

Welcome to a universe of gluten-free possibilities. How about we get baking!

Why a Bread Machine?

If you are new to gluten-free baking, you could ask why a bread machine is a particularly significant tool. The response is straightforward: it takes the mystery, exertion, and unpredictability out of the cycle, conveying amazing gluten-free portions easily. Bread machines offer accommodation, consistency, and control — three key variables while baking gluten-free bread at home.

1. Accommodation

A bread machine works on each step of the baking system. Whenever you've added the fixings, it handles everything: blending, plying, rising, and baking — across the board apparatus. This hands-off approach is great for occupied plans or for individuals who are new to baking. In addition, with preset settings explicitly for sans gluten bread, many machines are custom fitted to work with the special necessities of gluten-free batter.

2. Consistency

Sans gluten batter can be unpredictable. It doesn't rise and act the same way as batter made with customary flours, which can prompt conflicting outcomes while baking the hard way. A bread machine gives a controlled climate to the whole cycle — temperature, timing, and blending are completely computerized. This consistency guarantees that you obtain solid outcomes like clockwork, without having to screen the cycle physically.

3. Improved Texture and Rise

Since gluten-free mixture comes up short on flexibility of gluten, accomplishing the right texture and rise can be interesting. Bread machines ply the batter such that improves its structure, guaranteeing an even morsel and legitimate ascent. Many machines likewise offer a devoted sans gluten setting that changes the blending and rising times to suit gluten-free mixture, making a lighter, more breezy portion.

4. Controlled testing

A bread machine welcomes you to try different things with various recipes, flours, and flavor blends. Whether you need to attempt a basic gluten-free sandwich bread, a flavorful spice portion, or a sweet cinnamon raisin bread, the machine guarantees that every preliminary is essentially as simple as the last. You can investigate without the pressure of manual plying or stressing over consummating batter consistency.

5. Cost effective and Better Bread

Locally acquired gluten-free bread can be costly, and the fixings frequently incorporate additives, abundance sugar, and counterfeit added substances. With a bread machine, you have some control over everything goes into your bread. This implies better, more reasonable portions made with healthy, normal fixings that fit your dietary necessities.

To put it plainly, a bread machine removes the intricacy from sans gluten bread baking, offering steady, flavorful outcomes with insignificant exertion. It's the ideal apparatus to assist you with making pastry shop quality bread from the solace of your kitchen — without the wreck or fight!

Tips for gluten-free success

Baking gluten-free bread can feel precarious from the start, yet with the right methodology, you'll turn out delightful, reliable portions in a matter of seconds. Here are a few fundamental tips to assist you to prevail in your gluten-free bread-production venture:

1. Utilize a Mix of gluten-free Flours

No single sans gluten flour can completely replicate the properties of wheat flour, so it's essential to utilize a blend of various gluten-free flours. Popular options include rice flour, sorghum flour, almond flour, and tapioca starch. Combining these flours assists with enhancing texture and design for a better outcome. Numerous pre-blended gluten-free flour mixes are accessible, making this interaction significantly more straightforward.

2. Integrate binding agents

Since gluten-free flours don't have the regular restricting properties of gluten, it's vital to use binders like xanthan gum, guar gum or psyllium husk. These fixings assist with imitating gluten's flexibility, giving design and a superior ascent to your bread. Make certain to follow the recipe estimations intently, as adding excessively or too little can influence texture.

3. Measure Ingredients Cautiously

Accuracy is key in gluten-free baking. In contrast to ordinary bread recipes, where a slight difference in ingredients might be excused, sans gluten bread is more delicate. Continuously use estimating cups and spoons or, stunningly better, a kitchen scale to guarantee exactness. Little contrasts in flour or fluid sums can emphatically affect the result of your bread.

4. Add Water

Gluten-free bread batter is normally wetter and stickier than conventional mixture. This is typical and important to create delicate, cushioned bread. Gluten-free flours ingest more fluid, so don't be enticed to add more flour to make the batter less tacky — this will prompt a dry and brittle outcome. Adhere to the recipe's fluid to-flour proportions for best outcomes.

5. Allow the Mixture To rest

Gluten-free mixture frequently profits by resting prior to baking, which permits the flours to hydrate completely and works on the surface. Some bread machines have a "rest" cycle incorporated into their gluten-free settings, yet in the event that yours doesn't, you can stop the machine for 10-20 minutes subsequent to blending, prior to beginning the heat cycle.

6. Really take a look at Your Yeast

Make a point to utilize new, dynamic yeast. Gluten-free mixture depends vigorously on yeast for rise and design, so lapsed or latent yeast will bring about a thick, level portion. In the event that you're utilizing moment yeast or dynamic dry yeast, try to enact it in warm fluid (between 105-110°F) prior to including it.

7. Try not to Over-Blend

While gluten-free batter needs careful blending, over-blending can bring about a thick, weighty portion. Your bread machine is intended to work the batter suitably, yet on the off chance that you're blending the hard way or with a stand blender, be careful not to exhaust the mixture. Blend just until every one of the fixings are completely integrated.

8. Modify with caution

When you're alright with gluten-free bread recipes, you might need to explore different avenues regarding new flavors, grains, or add-ins like seeds, nuts, or dried natural products. While these increments can be heavenly, they can likewise modify the mixture's texture and rise, so begin by rolling out little improvements to a very much tried recipe.

9. Screen the Baking process

While your bread machine handles the greater part of the cycle, watch out for the batter as it blends. On the off chance that it looks excessively dry or excessively wet, you can make little changes — adding a tablespoon of water assuming, it's dry or a tablespoon of flour assuming that it's excessively sticky. This guarantees the right mixture consistency for baking.

10. Cool Bread Totally Prior to Cutting

After your bread is finished heating up, let it cool totally before cutting into it. Gluten-free bread needs time to set after it emerges from the machine. Cutting into it too soon can make the surface become sticky. Patience is critical —

hold on until the portion is completely cool for the best outcomes.

By following these tips, you'll get yourself in a position for gluten-free achievement! With training, you'll dominate the subtleties of sans gluten mixture and make tasty, pastry shop quality bread from your own kitchen.

Fundamental Elements for gluten-free Bread

With regards to baking sans gluten bread, it is essential to pick the right ingredients. Without gluten, you want a mix of flours and binders to imitate the texture, ascent, and versatility of conventional bread. Here is a breakdown of the fundamental fixings that will assist you with accomplishing heavenly, delicate, and very much organized gluten-free bread.

1. Gluten-free Flours

Since without gluten bread can't depend on wheat flour, you'll require a blend of elective flours. Each has various properties, so a mix is vital to repeating the texture of customary bread. Here are some normal gluten-free flours:

- Rice Flour: A staple in gluten-free baking, rice flour (both white and brown colored assortments) is impartial in flavor and light in surface. Earthy colored rice flour adds more supplements and a somewhat nuttier flavor.

- Sorghum Flour: Known for its gentle pleasantness, sorghum flour is much of the time used to upgrade flavor and give structure.

- Almond Flour: Produced using finely ground almonds, this flour adds dampness, flavor, and sound fats to sans gluten bread.

- Custard Starch: Separated from the cassava root, custard starch adds chewiness and assists give with breading a light, vaporous surface.

- Potato Starch: Not quite the same as potato flour, potato starch eases up the morsel and improves dampness.

- Millet Flour: This flour has a gentle, sweet flavor and makes a delicate morsel in gluten-free bread.

Numerous pre-made gluten-free flour mixes join these for a balanced base, however you can likewise make your own blend by trying different things with proportions.

2. Starches

Starches assist with imitating the flexibility and softness of gluten. They are imperative for making a delicate, chewy surface in sans gluten bread:

- Cornstarch: Frequently utilized for thickening and adding softness to heated merchandise.
- Arrowroot Starch: A flexible thickener, arrowroot gives bread a delicate surface.
- Custard Starch: As referenced, this starch adds stretchiness, assisting with emulating the chewiness of gluten.

3. Binders

Gluten-free bread comes up short on protein structure that keeps customary batter intact. To redress, you really want binders that give versatility and design. The most well-known choices are:

- Thickener: A famous binder, thickener helps keep the bread intact and gives it a superior ascent. It's essential in most gluten-free bread recipes.
- Guar Gum: Like thickener, guar gum is a characteristic thickener and cover produced using guar beans. An astounding option for those like to keep away from thickener.
- Psyllium Husk: Psyllium adds mass and fiber, and it shapes a gel-like consistency when blended in

with water, assisting with making a superior morsel structure. It's particularly valuable in gluten-free bread recipes to impersonate the versatility of gluten.

4. Leaveners

Leaveners are critical to aiding without gluten bread rise and accomplish a light, fluffy surface:

- Yeast: Very much like in conventional bread, yeast is fundamental for making gluten-free bread rise. Utilize either dynamic dry yeast or moment yeast (otherwise called quick ascent yeast), which is all the more normally utilized in bread machines. Yeast likewise adds flavor, so it's a vital element for both ascent and taste.

- Baking Powder and Baking soda: Some of the time utilized in mix with yeast, these assist with giving extra lift, particularly in fast breads or player batter based gluten-free recipes.

5. Liquid Ingredients

Gluten-free mixture needs more dampness than customary batter since sans gluten flours will generally be denser and softer. Key fluid fixings include:

- Water: The most well-known fluid used to hydrate the mixture and actuate yeast.
- Milk or Dairy-free Milk: Adds dampness, flavor, and wealth to the bread. Choices like almond milk, soy milk, or coconut milk function admirably for without dairy renditions.
- Eggs: Eggs give design, dampness, and extravagance. They additionally assist with raising. For veggie lover or without egg breads, flaxseed or chia seed "eggs" (a combination of ground seeds and water) can be utilized as substitutes.

6. Fats

Fats assist with making a delicate, tender crumb and add lavishness to gluten-free bread. They likewise hold the bread back from drying out excessively fast.

- Oil: Olive oil, vegetable oil, or dissolved coconut oil can be utilized to add dampness and flavor.
- Spread (or dairy-free Margarine): Adds wealth and assists with dampness maintenance in the bread.

7. Sweeteners

Sugars in bread aren't only for flavor — they additionally assist with enacting yeast and balancing the flavors in the bread.

- Sugar: A limited quantity of sugar or honey is frequently added to take care of the yeast and improve searing.
- Honey or Maple Syrup: These normal sugars can add flavor intricacy to your bread. Honey can also assist with making a more delicate piece.

8. Acidic Fixings

Adding a little corrosiveness can work on the texture of gluten-free bread by collaborating with the raising specialists to advance a superior ascent and scrap.

- Apple Juice Vinegar or Lemon Squeeze: A tablespoon or two of vinegar or lemon juice can assist with softening the batter and work on the rise, particularly when matched with baking powder or baking soda.

By getting it and utilizing these fundamental fixings, you'll be well headed to making gluten-free bread that rivals conventional portions in taste, texture, and satisfaction! Joining the right flours and binders will give you the apparatuses to accomplish wonderful gluten-free bread like clockwork.

Getting everything rolling with gluten-free Bread Machine Baking

Leaving on your gluten-free bread-production excursion can be both exciting and fulfilling. With a bread machine next to you, you can work on the cycle and accomplish steady, delightful outcomes with insignificant exertion. Here is a speedy manual to assist you with beginning on baking gluten-free bread with certainty.

1. Accumulate Your Ingredients

Before you start, guarantee you have every one of the fundamental fixings available. Stock up on an assortment of gluten-free flours, for example, rice flour, sorghum flour, and almond flour, alongside restricting specialists like thickener or psyllium husk. Remember to have yeast, fluids (like water or milk), fats (like oil or margarine), and sugars accessible. Having all that pre-arranged will make the baking process smoother and more enjoyable.

2. Pick the Right Recipe

Begin with a reliable gluten-free bread recipe that is explicitly intended for a bread machine. Search for recipes that give clear directions to the machine's settings, including the suitable flour mix and any binder required. As you gain insight, you can start to try different things with various flavors and ingredients.

3. Understand Your Bread Machine

Find out about your bread machine's settings and capabilities. Most machines have explicit projects for gluten-free bread, which change working and rising times to suit the one of a kind properties of gluten-free batter. Understanding how to utilize these elements will assist you with accomplishing improved results.

4. Follow Measurement Cautiously

Exactness is basic in gluten-free baking. Use estimating cups, spoons, or a kitchen scale to guarantee exact fixing amounts. Little varieties can essentially affect the texture and rise of your bread.

5. Screen the Blending System

As the bread machine blends the batter, pause for a minute to notice its consistency. Gluten-free mixture ought to be wetter and stickier than conventional batter. In the event that it looks excessively dry, you can add a tablespoon of water. This step guarantees that your bread will have a light and vaporous surface.

6. Show Patience

Permit your bread to cool totally subsequent to baking prior to cutting into it. Gluten-free bread frequently needs time to set, and cutting it too soon can bring about a sticky surface. Persistence is vital to partaking in the ideal cut off gluten-free bread.

7. Enjoy The Process!

Baking gluten-free bread at home is an excursion of investigation and inventiveness. Don't hesitate for even a moment to attempt new recipes, flavors, and strategies. Each portion you make will improve your abilities and extend your appreciation for gluten-free baking.

In light of these means, you're prepared to plunge into the universe of gluten-free bread machine baking. Embrace the experience, and before long you'll relish warm, natively constructed sans gluten bread right from your kitchen!

Picking the Right Flour: gluten-Free Options

Choosing the right flour is urgent in gluten-free baking, as various flours have particular properties that can fundamentally influence the surface, flavor, and construction of your bread. Here is a manual for probably the most popular gluten-free flours and their remarkable qualities to assist you with picking the best choices for your baking requirements.

1. Rice Flour

• Description: Accessible in both white and brown colored assortments, rice flour is a staple in gluten-free baking.

- Uses: It's impartial in flavor and can be utilized in various recipes, including bread, cakes, and treats.
- Properties: brown colored rice flour adds a marginally nuttier flavor and more fiber than white rice flour, settling on it a nutritious decision.

2. Sorghum Flour

- Description: Produced using the entire grain sorghum, this flour is somewhat sweet and adds a charming flavor to heated products.
- Uses: It's generally used in mixes for bread and pancakes.
- Properties: Sorghum flour works on the texture and adds dietary advantages, like protein and fiber.

3. Almond Flour

- Description: Ground from whitened almonds, almond flour is rich in sound fats and adds moisture to baked goods.
- Uses: Ideal for fast breads, treats, and biscuits.
- Properties: It has a somewhat sweet, nutty flavor and adds to a delicate, damp surface. Be that as it may, it tends to be denser than other gluten-free flours, so it's frequently joined with lighter flours.

4. Coconut Flour

- Description: Produced using dried coconut meat, coconut flour is high in fiber and has an unpretentious coconut flavor.

- Uses: Appropriate for treats, pancakes, and bread when used with care.

- Properties: Coconut flour retains a ton of moisture, so it's best utilized in blend with different flours and normally requires extra fluid or eggs in recipes.

5. Custard Starch

- Description: Extricated from the cassava root, custard starch is a fine white powder that gives chewiness and further develops surface.

- Uses: Ordinarily utilized in gluten-free flour mixes and for thickening sauces.

- Properties: It adds softness and can assist with making a dry outside in bread.

6. Potato Starch

- Description: Unique in relation to potato flour, potato starch is a fine white powder produced using the starch of potatoes.
- Uses: It's often used in sans gluten baking for its moisture holding properties and makes a delicate crump.
- Properties: Potato starch can add lightness and improve the texture of gluten-free breads.

7. Oat Flour

- Description: Produced using ground gluten-free oats, oat flour tastes gentle and is high in fiber.
- Uses: It functions admirably in hotcakes, biscuits, and breads.
- Properties: Oat flour can assist with working on the general surface and adds a somewhat sweet, healthy taste to heated bread goods. Guarantee you pick affirmed gluten-free oats to stay away from cross-contamination.

8. Chickpea Flour (Besan)

- Description: Produced using ground dried chickpeas, chickpea flour is high in protein and has a somewhat nutty flavor.
- Uses: It's perfect for making pancakes, flatbreads, and as a thickener.
- Properties: Chickpea flour can add thickness and a remarkable flavor to prepared products, settling on it a magnificent decision in mixes.

9. Millet Flour

- Description: Ground from the little grains of millet, this flour has a gentle, somewhat sweet flavor.
- Uses: It's reasonable for different heated baked goods and functions admirably in gluten-free flour mixes.
- Properties: Millet flour adds moisture and can assist with making a delicate crump, improving the general surface of the bread.

10. Gluten-free Flour Mixes

Numerous businesses sell gluten-free flour mixes are accessible that join a few of the above flours alongside starches and restricting specialists. These mixes are intended to emulate the properties of wheat flour and frequently include:

- Thickener or Guar Gum: For versatility and struture.
- Pre-estimated Proportions: These mixes are normally figured out to work on gluten-free baking, making them advantageous for amateurs.

By understanding the different sans gluten flour choices accessible, you can settle on informed decisions that will prompt fruitful and flavorful gluten-free baking. Each flour brings its own novel qualities, so go ahead and with various mixes to track down the ideal mix for your favorite recipes!

Understanding gluten-free Batter

Baking with gluten-free fixings requires an unexpected methodology in comparison to conventional baking. Since gluten, a protein tracked down in wheat, grain, and rye, gives batter its versatility and design, gluten-free mixture acts in an unexpected way. Understanding these distinctions is critical to effectively making gluten-free breads, cakes, and other heated products. Here is a more intensive gander at the qualities of sans gluten batter and how to really function with it.

1. Surface and Consistency

Gluten-free mixture will in general be more delicate and less versatile than customary batter because of the shortfall of gluten. Here are a few qualities to remember:

- Wet and sticky: gluten-free batter is many times wetter and stickier. This can make it challenging to deal with however is fundamental for accomplishing the right moisture content and surface in the end result.
- Thick and Dense: sans gluten batter might be denser than standard mixture. This thickness can

bring about a heavier bread or heated great, which is an interesting point while arranging your recipes.

2. Restricting Specialists

To emulate the design and flexibility that gluten gives, gluten-free recipes regularly require restricting specialists. These fixings assist with keeping the batter intact and make a positive surface:

- Thickener: This is possibly one of the most well-known restricting specialist utilized in gluten-free baking. It gives flexibility and dependability, permitting the batter to rise and hold its shape.
- Psyllium Husk: Another magnificent binder, psyllium husk adds fiber and dampness, working on the surface and rise of gluten-free baked product.
- Ground Chia or Flaxseeds: When blended in with water, these seeds make a gel-like substance that can go about as a limiting specialist, offering a more regular option.

3. Hydration Levels

Hydration assumes an essential part in gluten-free mixture:

- Higher Fluid Substance: gluten-free flours ingest fluids uniquely in contrast to wheat flour. You might have to build the fluid substance in your recipes to accomplish the ideal mixture consistency.
- Resting Period: Permitting the batter to rest subsequent to blending can assist with further developing hydration. This permits the flour to retain moisture completely, prompting better surface and design.

4. Rising and Fermentation

Gluten-free batter frequently requires different rising times and methods:

- Longer Rising Times: gluten-free mixture ordinarily profits by expanded rising periods. This creates flavor and takes into consideration better air pockets, adding to a lighter surface.
- Temperature Contemplations: Warm conditions can improve yeast action, assisting the mixture

with rising all the more. On the other hand, chilly temperatures can dial back fermentation.

5. Baking Strategies

Changing your baking strategies is fundamental for working with sans gluten mixture:

- Blending Strategy: gluten-free batters frequently require intensive blending to guarantee even appropriation of ingredients. Be that as it may, keep away from over mixing, as this can prompt a sticky surface.
- Forming: Because of its sticky nature, gluten-free mixture can be hard to shape. Rather than carrying it out, think about utilizing a greased spatula or wet hands to control the batter.
- Oven Temperature: Changing the baking temperature might be important. Gluten-free breads can profit from higher starting temperature to make a covering while at the same time keeping up with moisture inside.

By understanding the special properties of sans gluten batter, you can work on your baking methods and make flavorful, effective sans gluten heated merchandise. With training and trial and error, you'll track down the ideal mixes that work for your preferences and inclinations! Cheerful baking!

Common Pitfalls and How to avoid them in gluten-free Baking

Baking without gluten can be a rewarding yet testing try. Numerous bakers experience explicit pitfalls that can prompt disheartening outcomes. Understanding these normal errors and knowing how to stay away from them can fundamentally improve your gluten-free baking experience. Here is a manual for a few common pitfalls and tips to assist you with accomplishing delectable, effective gluten-free heated problem

1. Wrong Ingredients Measurement

Pitfalls: Exact estimations are critical in sans gluten baking. Utilizing excessively or excessively bit of a fixing can definitely change the texture and rise of your end result.

Solutions:

- Use a kitchen scale for exact estimations, particularly for gluten-free flours, which can change fundamentally in weight.

- Put resources into top notch estimating cups and spoons, and be aware of the difference between packed and loosed estimations.

2. Picking the wrong Flour

Pitfalls: Not all sans gluten flours are made equivalent. Utilizing some unacceptable flour or a flour that doesn't exactly measure up for the recipe can prompt unfortunate outcomes, like a thick or sticky texture.

Solutions:

- Look into different gluten-free flours and their properties. Joining various flours frequently yields the best outcomes.
- Use a pre-planned sans gluten flour mix explicitly intended for baking, which normally incorporates a blend of starches and entire grain flours.

3. Skipping Restricting Specialists

Pitfalls: gluten-free flours miss the mark on restricting properties of gluten, which can bring about brittle and dry prepared merchandise on the off chance that not tended to.

Solution:

- Continuously incorporate a limiting specialist, for example, thickener, psyllium husk, or ground chia seeds, in your recipes. These fixings assist with giving construction and versatility.
- Follow the suggested sums in recipes, as too minimal restricting specialist can prompt issues with surface.

4. Over-mixing or Under-mixing

Pitfall: Over mixing gluten-free batter can bring about a sticky surface, while under mixing can prompt uneven distribution of ingredients.

Solutions:

- Blend the mixture just until the ingredients are joined. This guarantees an even surface without overworking the mixture.
- For recipes that require air circulation, like cakes, make certain to adhere to the blending guidelines cautiously, as appropriate method can affect the end result.

5. Not Allowing Sufficient Rising Time

Pitfalls: gluten-free batter frequently requires longer rising times to appropriately create. Hurrying this cycle can prompt level and thick heated baked products.

Solution:

- Be patient and permit your mixture the chance to rise. Think about utilizing a warm climate to improve yeast movement.

6. Disregarding Cooling Times

Pitfalls: Cutting into gluten-free bread or prepared products too early can bring about a sticky surface and prevent proper crumb development.

Solution:

- Continuously let your heated products cool totally on a wire rack prior to cutting. This permits the design to set and works on the surface.
- Assuming you're making bread, stand by something like 30 minutes to an hour prior to cutting.

7. Not Using Fresh Fixings

Pitfall: Flat or terminated fixings, especially gluten-free flours and yeast, can adversely influence your baking outcomes.

Solution:

- Routinely check the expiring dates of your fixings, and store flours in sealed shut compartments in a cool, dry spot or in the fridge for longer timeframe of realistic usability.
- Continuously utilize new yeast and consider sealing it to guarantee its dynamic prior to adding it to your mixture.

8. Depending Too much on One Recipe

Pitfall: While it's perfect to find your most loved gluten-free bread recipe, depending entirely on it can restrict your abilities and results.

Solutions:

- Try different things with various recipes and methods to grow your gluten-free baking collection. This will assist you with understanding how different fixings cooperate and work on your general baking abilities.

- Take notes on what works and what doesn't, and change recipes according to your preference.

Basis gluten-free Bread Recipes

Baking gluten-free bread at home can be a satisfying and tasty experience. Whether you're following a gluten-free diet for wellbeing reasons or essentially investigating new culinary choices, having a couple of fundamental gluten-free bread recipes in your collection can have a significant effect. These recipes give a strong groundwork to gluten-free baking, offering a scope of flavors and textures that can take special care of different preferences and inclinations.

From delicate and cushioned portions to good and rural assortments, these basic gluten-free bread recipes are intended to be receptive for cooks of all ability levels. They utilize a mix of without gluten flours, restricting specialists, and straightforward procedures to assist you with making hand crafted bread that rivals customary assortments. Also, with the capacity to redo flavors and add-ins, you can undoubtedly fit every recipe to suit your own preferences.

Thus, focus in, accumulate your fixings, and prepare to partake in the magnificent smell of newly heated gluten-free bread drifting through your kitchen! Whether you're making an exemplary sandwich portion or exploring different avenues regarding spices and flavors, these recipes will direct you on your gluten-free baking excursion.

Classic White gluten-free Loaf

This Classic White Sans gluten Portion is ideal for sandwiches, toast, or just enjoying with a pat of butter. With its delicate, fluffy surface and gentle flavor, it's an incredible choice for anybody following a gluten-free diet. Simple to make and flexible, this bread will immediately become staple in your kitchen.

Ingredients

- 2 cups gluten-free regular flour (guarantee it contains thickener, or add 1 teaspoon if it doesn't)

- 2 tablespoon sugar or honey (for sweetness and to activate the yeast)

- 1 ½ tsp salt

- 1 ½ tsp active dry yeast or moment yeast (check without gluten status)

- 1 cup warm water (around 110°F or 43°C)

- ¼ cup olive oil or melted butter (adds moisture and lavishness)

- 2 huge eggs (room temperature; can substitute with flax eggs for a veggie lover choice)

Directions

1. Prepare the Bread Machine

Set your bread machine to the gluten-free setting if your machine has one. And if it doesn't, the basis or fast prepare setting typically functions well with gluten-free recipes, as these portions don't need broadened plying or different rises.

2. Add Wet Ingredients First

Pour the warm water, oil, eggs, and honey (if using) into the bread machine container. Blending wet ingredients first can help gluten-free batter mix up properly.

3. Add Dry Ingredients

Add the gluten-free flour, sugar (if used rather than honey), and salt on top of the wet fixings. Make a little hole in the middle of the flour and add the yeast. This keeps the yeast from activating too soon before the bread machine begins.

4. Start the Bread Machine

Select the appropriate setting and begin the bread machine. For gluten-free bread, a single rise is generally enough, so the machine ought to move directly from mixing to rising, and afterward to baking.

5. Monitor the Mixture Consistency

Around 5-10 minutes into the blending cycle, open the bread machine cover to actually look at the batter. It ought to be marginally sticky however keeping intact in a ball. If it's excessively dry, add warm water, 1 tablespoon at a time, until the batter arrives at the right consistency. In the event that it's excessively wet, add a little more flour.

6. Bake and Cool

When the baking cycle is finished, cautiously remove the bread dish from the machine. Allow the bread to cool in the pan for a few moments, then move it to a wire rack to totally cool. This helps maintain its texture and prevents a sticky surface.

7. Slice and Enjoy

Once completely cooled, cut your classic sans gluten portion and appreciate! This bread is ideally suited for sandwiches, toast, or basically as a nibble with spread or jam.

Simple Whole Grain gluten-free Bread

This Simple Whole Grain gluten-free Bread is a nutritious and good option in contrast to customary bread. Loaded with fiber and flavor, it's ideally suited for sandwiches, toast, or as a side for soups and salads. With basic fixings and direct guidelines, this recipe makes gluten-free baking available for everybody.

Fixings

- 1 ½ cups warm water (around 110°F or 43°C)

- ¼ cup olive oil or dissolved coconut oil

- 2 tbsp honey or maple syrup (optional for slight pleasantness)

- 2 huge eggs (room temperature; can substitute with flax eggs for veggie lover choice)

- 1 cup gluten-free oat flour

- 1 cup brown colored rice flour

- ½ cup sorghum flour

- ½ cup custard starch (assists with restricting and structure)

- ¼ cup ground flaxseed or chia seeds

- 1 ½ tsp salt

- 1 ½ tsp activate dry yeast or moment yeast (guarantee it's gluten-free)

Optional Add-ins for Additional and Flavor:

- ¼ cup sunflower seeds, pumpkin seeds, or sesame seeds

- 1-2 tbsp chia seeds or hemp seeds

Guidelines

1. Prepare the Bread Machine

Set your bread machine to the gluten-free setting, if available. If not, utilize the basis or speedy heat setting, as gluten-free bread requires less manipulating and just a single rise.

2. Add Wet Ingredients

In the bread machine dish, pour in the warm water, olive oil (or coconut oil), honey (if usesd), and eggs. Adding wet fixings first helps gluten-free batter mix properly.

3. Add Dry Ingredients

Add the oat flour, brown colored rice flour, sorghum flour, custard starch, ground flaxseed, and salt on top of the wet fixings. Make a little well in the middle of the flour and add the yeast to early keep it from enacting as well.

4. Start the Bread Machine

Select the gluten or basis bread cycle, then start the machine.

5. Check Batter Consistency

Around 5-10 minutes into the blending cycle, really take a look at the mixture. It ought to be thick and somehow sticky but a bit strong. In the event that it looks excessively dry, add a touch of more water, 1 tablespoon at a time. If it's excessively wet, sprinkle in some additional oat flour or custard starch.

6. Add Seeds (Optional)

If you have any desire to add seeds for additional texture, sprinkle them in once the batter has been mixed, before the bread begins rising.

7. Bake and Cool

At the point when the cycle finishes, remove the bread dish from the machine. Allow the bread to cool in the pan for 10 minutes, then move it to a wire rack to totally cool.

8. Slice and Enjoy

Once cooled, cut and enjoy your delicious whole grain gluten-free bread!

Soft and fluffy gluten-free Sandwich Bread

This Soft and Fluffy gluten-free Sandwich Bread is ideal for making delectable sandwiches, toasts, or enjoy alone with a bit of margarine or jam. Its light surface and gentle flavor makes it a great decision for families and anybody searching for a delightful gluten-free choice. With only a couple of straightforward fixings, you can make a superb portion that rivals customary bread.

Ingredients

- 1 ½ cups warm water (110°F or 43°C)
- ¼ cup olive oil or melted butter (for soft quality and flavor)
- 2 large eggs (room temperature; can substitute with flax eggs for vegetarian choice)
- 2 tbsp honey or sugar (to assist with browning and pleasantness)
- 2 ½ cups gluten-free regular baking flour mix (one that incorporates xanthan or guar gum for restricting; if not, add 1 tsp thickener)
- ½ cup custard starch (adds chewiness and softness)

- 1 tbsp apple cider vinegar (improves mixture rise and soft quality)
- 1 ½ tsp salt
- 1 tbsp active dry yeast or instant yeast (ensure its gluten-free)

Directions

1. Set up the Bread Machine

Set your bread machine to the gluten-free setting. If it doesn't have one, use the basis or fast heat setting. Gluten-free bread just needs one rise.

2. Add Wet Fixings

Pour the warm water, olive oil, eggs, honey (or sugar), and apple cider vinegar into the bread machine container. Adding wet fixings first can help gluten-free batters mix properly.

3. Add Dry Fixings

Add the gluten-free regular baking flour mix, custard starch, and salt on top of the wet fixings. Make a little well in the middle of the flour and add the yeast, keeping it separate from the salt and fluids to avoid untimely activation.

4.   Start the Bread Machine

Begin the bread machine on the gluten-free or basis setting.

5.   Check the Mixture Consistency

Around 5-10 minutes into the mixing cycle, really look at the batter's consistency. It would be ideal for it to be thick yet somewhat sticky. If it's excessively dry, add a tablespoon of warm water at a time until it reaches the right consistency. If it's excessively wet, add a little more gluten-free flour mix.

6.   Allow it To rise and Bake

The bread machine will deal with the rise and bake time. When gotten done, the bread ought to have a brilliant top and a delicate, breezy surface.

7.   Cool Totally

Remove the bread container from the machine, permitting the portion to cool for a couple of moments in the dish prior to moving it to a wire rack. Allow it to cool totally before cutting for the best surface.

8.   Cut and AppreciateWhen cooled, this delicate, soft portion is ideally suited for sandwiches, toast, from there, the sky is the limit!

Dairy free gluten-free Bread

This dairy-free gluten-free Bread is a flexible and healthy choice for those keeping away from dairy items. With a delicate surface and rich flavor, it's ideal for sandwiches, toast, or just enjoying with a spread. Easy to make and delectable, this recipe will fit flawlessly into your gluten-free, dairy-free way of life.

Fixings

- 1 ½ cups warm water (around 110°F or 43°C)
- ¼ cup dairy-free oil, (for example, olive oil or liquefied coconut oil)
- 2 tbsp maple syrup (a tad of pleasantness and to activate the yeast)
- 2 enormous eggs (room temperature; for a veggie lover variant, utilize 2 flax eggs: 2 tbsp ground flaxseed blended in with 6 tbsp water)
- 2 ½ cups gluten-free regular flour mix (one that incorporates xanthan or guar gum; if not, add 1 tsp thickener)
- ½ cup brown colored rice flour (adds a subtle nutty flavor)

- ¼ cup custard starch (assists with restricting and soft quality)
- 1 ½ tsp salt
- 1 tbsp apple cider vinegar (further improves rise and texture)
- 1 ½ tsp dynamic dry yeast or instant yeast (guarantee it's sans gluten)

Guidelines

1. Set up the Bread Machine

Set your bread machine to the gluten-free settings if available. If not, use the basic or fast heat setting, as gluten-free breads only need just a single rise.

2. Add Wet Fixings

Pour the warm water, oil, maple syrup (or honey), eggs (or flax eggs), and apple cider vinegar into the bread machine pan. Adding wet fixings first helps gluten-free batters mix well.

3. Add Dry Fixings

Add the gluten-free regular flour mix, brown colored rice flour, custard starch, and salt on top of the wet fixings. Make a little well in the middle of the flour and add the yeast to keep it from activating

4.   Start the Bread Machine

Select the gluten-free or basic setting and start the machine.

5.   Check Your Batter Consistency

Around 5-10 minutes into the mixing cycle, open the top to actually take a look at the mixture. It ought to be thick and marginally tacky yet kept in a smooth ball. If it's excessively dry, add a tablespoon of warm water at a time; if too wet, add a bit more gluten-free flour mix.

6.   Allow It To rise and Heat

Permit the bread machine to deal with the rise and baking cycle. The completed bread ought to be brilliant brown on top with a delicate, breezy inside.

7.   Cool Totally

When the cycle is finished, remove the dish from the machine and let the bread cool for a couple of moments. Then, at that point, move it to a wire rack to cool totally prior to cutting, which helps hold the bread back from becoming sticky.

8.   Cut and Appreciate

Enjoy this soft, dairy-free, gluten-free bread for sandwiches, toast, or any meal

Basic Veggie lover gluten-free Loaf

This Basis Veggie lover gluten-free loaf is a basic and nutritious choice that everybody can appreciate. Ideal for sandwiches, toast, or as a side to your soups and salads, this portion is light, fluffy, and totally plant-based. With a couple of staple fixings, you can make a delightful gluten-free bread that accommodates your dietary necessities.

Fixings

- 1 ½ cups warm water (around 110°F or 43°C)
- ¼ cup olive oil (adds moisture and flavor)
- 1 tbsp apple cider vinegar (works on the surface and rise)
- 2 enormous eggs (room temperature; can substitute with flax eggs for a veggie lover choice: 2 tbsp ground flaxseed blended in with 6 tbsp water)

- 2 ½ cups gluten-free regular flour mix (one with xanthan or guar gum; in the event that not, add 1 tsp thickener)
- ½ cup custard starch (for restricting and chewiness)
- 1 tsp salt
- 1 tbsp sugar or maple syrup (to assist with activating the yeast)
- 1 ½ tsp dynamic dry yeast or active yeast (guarantee it's gluten-free)

Veggie Add-Ins (Pick 1-2, around ½ cup total)

- ½ cup destroyed carrots
- ½ cup finely chopped bell peppers (drain excess moisture)
- ¼ cup chopped spinach (press remove excess fluid)
- ¼ cup finely chopped zucchini (lightly squeeze to remove excess fluid)
- ¼ cup chopped green onions or leeks
- 1-2 tbsp chopped new spices (like basil, parsley, or rosemary) for additional flavor

Guidelines

1. Set up the Bread Machine

Set your bread machine to the gluten-free setting if has one, or utilize the basic or fast bake setting, as gluten-free breads usually needs to rise just once.

2.   Add Wet Fixings

Pour the warm water, olive oil, eggs (or flax eggs), and apple cider vinegar into the bread machine pan. Adding wet fixings first assists the batter mix well.

3.   Add Dry Fixings

Add the gluten-free regular baking flour, custard starch, salt, and sugar on top of the wet fixings. Make a little hole in the middle of the flour and add the yeast to prevent early activation.

4.   Add Vegetables and Spices

Sprinkle your picked veggies and spices into the bread dish on top of the dry fixings. Abstain from adding excessively, as excess moisture from vegetables can affect the batter's texture.

5.   Start the Bread Machine

Select the gluten-free or essential setting and turn on the bread machine.

6.   Check Mixture Consistency

Following 5-10 minutes of mixing, take a look at the batter. It ought to be thick and somewhat sticky. If its excessively dry, add warm water, 1 tablespoon at a time; if too wet, add a little more gluten-free flour.

7.   Heat and Cool

Permit the bread machine to finish the baking cycle. The portion ought to have a brilliant brown colored crust and soft texture inside.

8.   Cool and Cut

Remove the bread from the pan and cool on a wire rack. Allow it to cool totally prior to cutting to keep away from a sticky surface.

9.   Appreciate

Serve your veggie darling's portion as a flavorful sandwich bread, toasted with spreads, or as a backup to soups and salads!

Savory gluten-free Bread Recipes

Savory gluten-free breads are an incredible way of bringing rich, generous flavors to your baking. From spice imbued portions to vegetable-pressed choices, these breads add a heavenly wind to regular dinners. Ideal for sandwiches, toasts, or as a delightful side, savory gluten-free breads pair wonderfully with a scope of dishes. Ingredients like garlic, rosemary, olives, or sun-dried tomatoes raise each portion, making these breads ideal for those looking for gluten-free choices without compromising taste. Whether you're heating up a delicate sandwich bread or a dry craftsman portion, these flavorful recipes are sure to please!

Spice and Garlic gluten-free Bread

This Spice and Garlic gluten-free Bread is a fragrant and tasty expansion to any feast. Overflowing with the essence of new spices and simmered garlic, it's ideal for serving close by soups, mixed greens, or as a base for tasty sandwiches. This recipe is easy to make and will fill your kitchen with a superb fragrance as it bakes.

Fixings

- 1 ½ cups warm water (around 110°F or 43°C)
- ¼ cup olive oil (adds moisture and flavor)
- 1 tbsp honey (just a little of pleasantness and to assist the yeast with activating)
- 2 enormous eggs (room temperature; can substitute with flax eggs for a vegetarian choice)
- 2 ½ cups gluten-free regular baking flour mix (one with xanthan or guar gum; if not, add 1 tsp thickener)
- ½ cup custard starch (assists with binding and chewiness)
- 1 ½ tsp salt
- 1 tbsp apple cider vinegar (further develops texture and rise)
- 1 tbsp dynamic dry yeast or active yeast (ensure it's gluten-free)

Seasonings

- 2-3 cloves garlic, minced (or 1-2 tsp garlic powder)
- 1 tbsp dried Italian spices (or a blend of basil, oregano, and thyme)
- ½ tsp dark pepper

- ½ tsp smoked paprika (for a bit of smokiness)
- 1 tbsp new rosemary or thyme, slashed (optional, for added fragrance)

Guidelines

1. Set up the Bread Machine

Set your bread machine to the gluten-free setting if availiable. If not, utilize the basic or speedy heat setting, as gluten-free bread commonly needs only one rise.

2. Add Wet Fixings

Pour the warm water, olive oil, eggs (or flax eggs), honey, and apple cider vinegar into the bread machine. Adding wet fixings first aids gluten-free batters blend properly.

3. Add Dry Fixings

Add the gluten-free regular flour mix, custard starch, salt, and yeast on top of the wet fixings.

4. Add Flavors

Sprinkle the garlic, Italian spices, dark pepper, smoked paprika, and new spices (if used) into the bread machine container. Conveying the flavors all through the flour assists them with blending uniformly.

5.   Start the Bread Machine

Select the gluten-free or essential setting and start the machine.

6.   Check Batter Consistency

Following 5-10 minutes, take a look at the mixture. It ought to be thick and marginally sticky however keeping intact. If it's excessively dry, add a tablespoon of warm water at a time. If it's excessively wet, sprinkle in some more gluten-free flour.

7.   Prepare and Cool

Allow the bread machine to finish the baking cycle. The portion ought to be brilliant brown with a delectably fragrant outside.

8.   Cool Totally

Remove the bread from the pan and put it on a wire rack to cool totally prior to cutting. Cooling keeps up with the bread's surface.

9.   Cut and Appreciate

Once cooled, enjoy this delightful, fragrant bread with soups, as toast, or essentially all alone!

Gluten-free Olive Bread

This gluten-free Olive Bread is an exquisite joy, ideal for the individuals who love the rich taste of olives. With a delicate and sodden morsel, this bread pairs wonderfully with cheddar, charcuterie, or as a backup to soups and mixed greens. Whether you appreciate it new or toasted, this recipe is easy to make and an incredible expansion to your gluten-free baking collection.

Fixings

- 1 ½ cups warm water (around 110°F or 43°C)
- ¼ cup olive oil (adds moisture and upgrades the olive flavor)
- 1 tbsp honey or sugar (activate the yeast and adds a sprinkle of pleasantness)
- 2 huge eggs (room temperature; can substitute with flax eggs for a vegetarian choice)
- 2 ½ cups gluten-free regular baking flour mix (guarantee it contains xanthan or guar gum; if not, add 1 tsp thickener)
- ½ cup custard starch (assists with restricting and chewiness)

- 1 ½ tsp salt
- 1 tbsp apple cider vinegar (further develops texture and rise)
- 1 tbsp dynamic dry yeast or active yeast (guarantee it's gluten-free)

Olive and Spice Blend

- ½ cup pitted and chopped olives (Kalamata or green olives works well; drain excess fluid)
- 1 tbsp new rosemary or thyme, finely chopped (optional)
- ½ tsp garlic powder or 1 little clove garlic, minced (optional for added flavor)

Guidelines

1. Set up the Bread Machine

Set your bread machine to the gluten-free setting if it has one, or uses the basis or fast prepare setting.

2. Add Wet Fixings

Pour the warm water, olive oil, eggs (or flax eggs), honey, and apple cider vinegar into the bread machine pan. Adding wet fixings first aids gluten-free batters blend perfectly.

3.   Add Dry Fixings

Add the gluten-free regular flour mix, custard starch, salt, and yeast on top of the wet fixings. Creating a little well in the flour for the yeast can assist it with remaining separate until mixing starts.

4.   Add Olives and Spices

Sprinkle the chopped olives, rosemary (if utilizing), and garlic powder over the flour. Adding these blend toward the beginning permits the bread machine to integrate them equally into the mixture.

5.   Start the Bread Machine

Select the gluten-free or basic setting and start the machine.

6.   Check The Mixture Consistency

Around 5-10 minutes into the blending cycle, take a look at the batter. It ought to be thick and somewhat sticky yet firm. In the event that it appears to be excessively dry, add warm water, 1 tablespoon at a time; if too wet, add a little more gluten-free flour mix.

7.   Prepare and Cool

Allow the bread machine to finish its baking cycle. The portion ought to have a brilliant earthy colored outside layer with a delicate inside and sweet-smelling, herby fragrance.

8.   Cool Totally

Remove the bread from the dish and let it cool on a wire rack prior to cutting to guarantee the best texture.

9.   Cut and Appreciate

Once cooled, enjoy this tasty olive bread with soups, as a sandwich, or as a flavorful snack!

Sun-Dried Tomato and Basil gluten-free Bread

This Sun-Dried Tomato and Basil Without gluten Bread is a delightful portion that catches the quintessence of Mediterranean food. Overflowing with the rich taste of sun-dried tomatoes and the sweet-smelling newness of basil, this bread is ideally suited for presenting with soups, mixed greens, or as a base for sandwiches. It's easy to make and adds a magnificent curve to your gluten-free baking assortment.

Fixings

- 1 ½ cups warm water (around 110°F or 43°C)

¼ cup olive oil (for dampness and flavor)

- 1 tbsp honey or sugar (to assist with activating the yeast)
- 2 enormous eggs (room temperature; can substitute with flax eggs for a vegetarian choice)
- 2 ½ cups sans gluten regular flour mix (with xanthan or guar gum included; if not, add 1 tsp thickener)
- ½ cup custard starch (for restricting and chewiness)

- 1 ½ tsp salt
- 1 tbsp apple cider vinegar (further develops rise and texture)
- 1 tbsp dynamic dry yeast or active yeast (guarantee it's gluten-free)

Sun-Dried Tomato and Basil Blend

- ½ cup sun-dried tomatoes, finely chopped (use oil-stuffed and pat off, or rehydrate dried ones in warm water and drain)
- 2 tbsp new basil, finely cleaved (or 1 tbsp dried basil)
- ½ tsp garlic powder (optional, for an savory kick)
- 1 tsp Italian seasoning or dried oregano (optional, to upgrade Mediterranean flavor)

Directions

1. Set up the Bread Machine

Set your bread machine to the gluten-free setting in the event that it has one; if not, use the essential or fast setting, as gluten-free breads need just a single rise.

2. Add Wet Fixings

Pour the warm water, olive oil, eggs (or flax eggs), honey, and apple cider vinegar into the bread machine pan .starting with wet fixings assists the batter with blending efficiently.

3.   Add Dry Fixings

Add the gluten-free regular baking flour mix, custard starch, salt, and yeast to the pan. Making a little well in the flour for the yeast can forestall untimely activation.

4.   Add Sun-Dried Tomato and Basil Blend

Add the chopped sun-dried tomatoes, basil, garlic powder, and Italian flavoring on top of the dry fixings.

5.   Start the Bread Machine

Select the gluten-free or fundamental setting and turn on the machine.

6.   Really take a look at Mixture Consistency

After around 5-10 minutes of blending, really take a look at the mixture's consistency. It ought to be thick and marginally sticky however firm. If excessively dry, add a touch of warm water, 1 tablespoon at a time. If excessively wet, add more gluten-free flour.

7. Bake and Cool

Permit the bread machine to finish its baking cycle. The portion ought to have a brilliant outside layer and soft with pockets of tomato and basil all through.

8. Cool Totally

When the baking cycle is finished, remove the bread from the dish and cool it on a wire rack. This will assist with forestalling a sticky surface and make it simpler to cut.

9. Cut and Appreciate

Once cooled, cut and enjoy in this tasty portion with servings of mixed greens, as sandwich bread, or with your favorite Mediterranean feasts!

Savory Cheese Bread (dairy-free Choice)

This Exquisite Cheese Bread is a delightfully fluffy portion that carries an eruption of flavor to your table. With a blend of flavorful spices and a messy taste, this gluten-free bread is ideally suited for sandwiches, toast, or as a wonderful side for soups and mixed greens. Furthermore, it incorporates a dairy-free choice, making it open for everybody to enjoy!

Fixings

- 1 ½ cups warm water (around 110°F or 43°C)
- ¼ cup olive oil (adds moisture and flavor)
- 1 tbsp maple syrup or sugar (activate the yeast and adds a touch of sweetness)
- 2 enormous eggs (room temperature; or 2 flax eggs for a veggie lover choice: 2 tbsp ground flaxseed blended in with 6 tbsp water)
- 2 ½ cups gluten-free regular flour mix (guarantee it incorporates xanthan or guar gum; if not, add 1 tsp thickener)
- ½ cup tapioca starch (just a little of chewiness and restricting)

- 1 ½ tsp salt
- 1 tbsp apple cider vinegar (further develops surface and rise)
- 1 tbsp dynamic dry yeast or active yeast (guarantee it's gluten-free)

Dairy-free Cheese and Preparing Mix

- ½ cup shredded dairy-free cheese (cheese or mozzarella-style for the best flavor)
- ½ tsp garlic powder (optional, for additional flavor)
- ½ tsp smoked paprika (adds a hint of smokiness)
- 1 tbsp new chives or parsley, finely chopped (optional, for color and flavor)

Guidelines

1. Set up the Bread Machine

Set your bread machine to the gluten-free setting if available. If not, use the essential or fast heat setting, as sans gluten breads commonly need just a single rise.

2. Add Wet Fixings

Pour the warm water, olive oil, eggs (or flax eggs), maple syrup, and apple cider vinegar into the bread machine pan. Adding the wet fixings first assists with blending.

3.   Add Dry Fixings

Add the gluten-free regular baking flour, custard starch, salt, and yeast on top of the wet fixings. Creating a little well in the flour for the yeast can help with keeping it dry until blending starts.

4.   Add dairy-free Cheese and Flavors

Sprinkle the shredded dairy-free cheese, garlic powder, smoked paprika, and chives on top of the dry fixings. Distributing the seasonings all through the flour assists them with mixing uniformly.

5.   Start the Bread Machine

Select the gluten-free or basic setting and start the machine.

6.   Check Mixture Consistency

After around 5-10 minutes of blending, Take a look at the batter. It would be ideal for it to be thick and somehow sticky yet strong. In the event that the batter excessively dry, add a tablespoon of warm water at a time. If excessively wet, sprinkle in more sans gluten flour mix.

7.   Bake and Cool

Permit the bread machine to finish the baking cycle. The portion ought to come out brilliant with a delicate, cushioned inside and savory cheese flavor all through.

8.   Cool Totally

When the baking cycle is finished, remove the bread from the container and let it cool on a wire rack prior to cutting.

9.   Cut and Serve

Once cooled, enjoy this exquisite, cheesy loafs with soups, as a sandwich bread, or toasted with your favorite spreads.

Sweet Sans gluten Bread Recipes

Sweet gluten-free bread recipes offer a great method for reveling your desires while observing dietary limitations. Whether you're searching for a soft banana bread, a rich cinnamon swirl loaf, or a fruity speedy bread, these recipes give a scope of flavors and textures to fulfill any sweet tooth.

Baking sweet gluten-free bread at home permits you to control the ingredients as well as allows you to explore different avenues regarding different gluten-free flours, regular sugars, and add-ins like nuts, chocolate chips, or dried natural products. These breads are ideally suited for breakfast, bites, or even as a unique treat to with loved ones.

As well as being flavorful, large numbers of these recipes are not difficult to make and can be adjusted to be dairy-free or vegetarian, guaranteeing everybody can partake in a cut. Along these lines, set up your bread machine, assemble your fixings, and prepare to heat some luscious sweet gluten-free breads that will fill your home with brilliant smells and leave everybody requesting for more!

Cinnamon Raisin gluten-free Bread

This Cinnamon Raisin gluten-free Bread is a warm, consoling portion that fills your kitchen with the brilliant smell of cinnamon and sugar. It's ideally suited for breakfast, as a bite, or even toasted with a pat of margarine or a spread of choice. This bread isn't just gluten-free but also additionally unquestionably simple to make, guaranteeing that everybody can enjoy in a cut of this classic favorite!

Fixings

- 1 ½ cups warm water (around 110°F or 43°C)
- ¼ cup oil (softened coconut oil or vegetable oil)
- ¼ cup honey or maple syrup (adds natural sweetness)
- 2 enormous eggs (room temperature; can substitute with flax eggs for a veggie lover choice: 2 tbsp ground flaxseed + 6 tbsp water)
- 2 ½ cups gluten-free regular flour mix (guarantee it incorporates xanthan or guar gum; if not, add 1 tsp thickener)
- ½ cup custard starch (for restricting and chewiness)
- 1 ½ tsp salt

- 1 tbsp apple cider vinegar (assists with texture and rise)
- 1 tbsp dynamic dry yeast or instant yeast (guarantee it's gluten-free)

Cinnamon and Raisin Blend

- ½ cup raisins (or dried currants; soaked in warm water for 10 minutes and drained)
- 1 ½ tbsp ground cinnamon
- 1 tbsp sugar (optional, for additional pleasantness and flavor)

Guidelines

1. Set up the Bread Machine

Set your bread machine to the gluten-free setting, or if it doesn't have one, utilize the basic or speedy bake setting, as gluten-free bread just requires one rise.

2. Add Wet Fixings

Pour the warm water, oil, eggs (or flax eggs), honey, and apple cider vinegar into the bread machine dish. Adding wet fixings helps assists with mixing.

3.   Add Dry Fixings

Add the gluten-free regular baking flour, custard starch, salt, and yeast on top of the wet fixings. Creating a little well in the flour for the yeast can assist it with remaining dry until mixing starts.

4.   Add Cinnamon and Raisins

Sprinkle the cinnamon and raisins over the dry fixings. This will assist with distributing them equally all through the batter as it blends.

5.   Start the Bread Machine

Select the gluten-free or basic setting and begin the machine.

6.   Check Mixture Consistency

After around 5-10 minutes, take a look at the mixture's consistency. It ought to be thick, somewhat sticky, and keep intact. If excessively dry, add warm water, 1 tablespoon at a time. If too wet, add somewhat more gluten-free flour.

7.   Bake and Cool; Allow the bread machine to finish its baking cycle. The bread ought to come out with a brilliant outside layer and a warm, flavored aroma.

8.   Cool Totally

Once done, remove the bread from the dish and put it on a wire rack to cool totally prior to cutting. Cooling guarantees the bread sets properly

9.   Cut and Enjoy

Once cooled, cut and enjoy in your cinnamon raisin bread toasted with margarine, spread with nut butter, or simply as it is.

Gluten-free Chocolate Chip Brioche

This gluten-free Chocolate Chip Brioche is a soft, rich, and somewhat sweet bread with pockets of rich chocolate chips dispersed all through. Ideal for a wanton breakfast, snacks, dessert, this gluten-free variant of an exemplary brioche keeps up with the sumptuous texture and flavor, all while being suitable for gluten-free diets. The batter is improved with eggs and a sprinkle of sweetness, making every bite satisfying and fulfilling.

Fixings

- ¾ cup warm milk of choice (around 110°F or 43°C; almond, oat, or cow's milk works well)
- ¼ cup melted butter or dairy-free spread
- ¼ cup sugar or honey
- 3 enormous eggs (room temperature)
- 1 tsp vanilla extract
- 2 ½ cups gluten-free regular flour mix (guarantee it contains xanthan or guar gum; if not, add 1 tsp thickener)
- ½ cup custard starch (for texture and softness)
- 1 ½ tsp salt

- 1 tbsp dynamic dry yeast or instant yeast (guarantee it's gluten-free)
- ½ cup dairy-free or normal chocolate chips (or smaller than usual chocolate chips for even distribution)

Guidelines

1. Set up the Bread Machine

Set your bread machine to the gluten-free setting if available. If not, utilize the fundamental or fast bake setting, as gluten-free breads regularly need just a single rise.

2. Add Wet Fixings

Pour the warm milk, melted butter, sugar, eggs, and vanilla extract into the bread machine pan.

3. Add Dry Fixings

Add the gluten-free flour mix, custard starch, salt, and yeast on top of the wet fixings. Making a little well in the flour for the yeast help keep it dry until mixing starts.

4. Add Chocolate Chips

Sprinkle the chocolate chips over the dry fixings. This will assist with distributing them uniformly all through the batter as it blends.

5. Start the Bread Machine

Select the gluten-free or basic setting and turn on the machine.

6. Check your Batter Consistency

After around 5-10 minutes, actually take a look at the mixture's consistency. It would be ideal for it to be soft and marginally sticky. If it's excessively dry, add a little more warm milk, 1 tablespoon at a time. If excessively wet, sprinkle in a touch more gluten-free flour.

7. Bake and Cool

Permit the bread machine to finish the baking cycle. The brioche ought to come out brilliant with a soft, fleecy inside and pockets of melted chocolate chips.

8. Cool Totally

Remove the brioche from the container and let it cool on a wire rack prior to cutting to prevent crumbling.

9.   Cut and Enjoy

Once cooled, cut and enjoy this chocolate chip brioche with a touch of margarine or all alone as a flavorful, sweet treat!

Honey Oat gluten-free Bread

This Honey Oat gluten-free Bread is a healthy, somewhat sweet portion with a good surface and the nutty kind of oats. Ideal for sandwiches, toast, or presented with margarine and jam, this bread carries a rural appeal to any feast. The blend of honey and oats makes a soothing, feeding portion that is perfect for breakfast or as a dessert, and it's completely gluten-free!

Fixings

- 1 ½ cups warm water (around 110°F or 43°C)
- ¼ cup olive oil or liquefied coconut oil
- ¼ cup honey (or maple syrup for a vegetarian choice)
- 2 huge eggs (room temperature; or 2 flax eggs: 2 tbsp ground flaxseed + 6 tbsp water)
- 2 ½ cups gluten-free regular flour mix (guarantee it incorporates xanthan or guar gum; if not, add 1 tsp thickener)
- ½ cup gluten-free oat flour (adds nutty flavor and surface)
- ½ cup gluten-free rolled oats (for added surface; hold a couple for sprinkling on top)

- 1 ½ tsp salt

- 1 tbsp apple cider vinegar (further improves rise and surface)

- 1 tbsp dynamic dry yeast or instant yeast (guarantee it's gluten-free)

Guidelines

1. Set up the Bread Machine

Set your bread machine to the gluten-free setting if available. If not, utilize the essential or speedy bake setting, as gluten-free breads need just a single rise.

2. Add Wet Fixings

Pour the warm water, olive oil, honey, eggs (or flax eggs), and apple cider vinegar into the bread machine pan.

3. Add Dry Fixings

Add the gluten-free regular flour mix, oat flour, rolled oats, and salt on top of the wet fixings.

4. Add Yeast

Make a little well in the dry fixings and add the yeast on top. This helps keep the yeast dry until blending starts.

5.   Start the Bread Machine

Select the gluten-free or basic setting and start the machine.

6.   Check Mixture Consistency

After around 5-10 minutes, look at the batter's consistency. It ought to be thick and somewhat sticky but well mixed. if it's excessively dry, add more warm water, 1 tablespoon at a time. If excessively wet, add a bit more gluten-free flour.

7.   Sprinkle with Oats

Subsequent to mixing, sprinkle a couple of saved rolled oats over the batter if you'd like a decorative touch on your loaf.

8.   Bake and Cool

Allow the bread machine to finish its baking cycle. The loaf ought to emerge with a brilliant outside and a soft, slightly chewy inside.

9.   Cool Totally

Remove the bread from the container and let it cool on a wire rack. Cooling completely guarantees it cuts well and the surface sets appropriately.

10.   Cut and Enjoy

Once cooled, cut and enjoy this honey oat bread as toast, sandwich bread, or with your number one spread.

Banana Nut gluten-free Bread (Vegetarian Choice)

This Banana Nut Sans gluten Bread is clammy, delightful, and loaded with the regular sweetness of ripe bananas and the smash of toasted nuts. With no dairy or eggs, an ideal vegetarian choice actually conveys a delicate, heavenly portion. Incredible for breakfast, a bite, or even treat, this banana bread is not difficult to make and brimming with healthy fixings that everybody can enjoy.

Fixings

- 1 cup squashed ripe bananas (around 2-3 bananas)
- ½ cup milk of choice (almond, oat, or customary milk)
- ¼ cup olive oil or liquefied coconut oil
- ¼ cup honey or maple syrup
- 2 huge eggs (room temperature; or 2 flax eggs for a veggie lover choice: 2 tbsp ground flaxseed + 6 tbsp water)
- 1 ½ cups gluten-free regular flour mix (guarantee it incorporates xanthan or guar gum; if not, add 1 tsp thickener)

- ½ cup almond flour (adds moisture and a subtle nutty flavor)
- 1 tsp baking powder
- ½ tsp baking soda
- ½ tsp salt
- ½ tsp ground cinnamon
- ½ cup chopped pecans or walnuts (reserve a couple for sprinkling on top)

Guidelines

1. Set up the Bread Machine

Set your bread machine to thesans gluten setting if available. If not, utilize the fast bread or cake setting to prevent over-mixing.

2. Add Wet Fixings

Add the crushed bananas, milk, oil, honey (or maple syrup), and eggs (or flax eggs) to the bread machine container.

3. Add Dry Fixings

On top of the wet fixings, add the gluten-free flour mix, almond flour, baking powder, baking pop, salt, and cinnamon.

4. Add Nuts

Sprinkle the cleaved nuts over the dry fixings reserve a couple of pieces to sprinkle on top for enrichment.

5. Start the Bread Machine

Select the gluten-free or speedy bread setting and start the machine. This bread doesn't have to rise, so a shorter baking time is great.

6. Check Mixture Consistency

Following 5-10 minutes of blending, Take a look at the consistency of the dough. It ought to be thick however pourable, similar to a biscuit batter. If excessively thick, add a little more milk, 1 tablespoon at a time. If excessively soft, add a touch more almond flour.

7. Sprinkle with Nuts

Sprinkle the saved nuts over the batter for added crunch and decoration.

8. Bake and Cool

Remove the bread machine to finish its baking cycle. The banana nut bread ought to come out brilliant and marginally domed on top.

9.   Cool Totally

Remove the bread from the pan and let it cool on a wire rack prior to cutting. This helps the bread set and guarantees simple cutting.

10.   Cut and Enjoy

Once cooled, cut and enjoy this banana nut bread as a sweet breakfast, snack, or even dessert.

Gluten-free Bread for Special Eating Diets

Gluten-free bread for unique weight control plans takes special care of a wide assortment of dietary necessities, guaranteeing that everybody can appreciate tasty, homemade bread without compromising on wellbeing or taste. Whether you follow a vegan, dairy-free, low-sugar, or paleo way of life, there are recipes customized to meet these particular requirements. These breads integrate elective flours, sugars, and dairy substitutes while keeping up with extraordinary texture and flavor. From keto-friendly loaves to allergen-free choices, gluten-free bread for extraordinary weight control plans permits anybody to appreciate new, hand crafted bread that lines up with their novel wellbeing necessities.

Low-Carb gluten-free Bread

This Low-Carb gluten-free Bread is ideal for those following a low-carb or keto way of life while keeping away from gluten. Made with supplement thick fixings like almond flour and flaxseeds, this bread is an extraordinary option in contrast to conventional high-carb portions. It's soft, slightly thick, and loaded with flavor, making it ideal for sandwiches, toast, or a side to your favorite feasts.

Fixings

- 1 cup warm water (around 110°F or 43°C)
- ¼ cup olive oil or softened coconut oil
- 3 enormous eggs (room temperature)
- 1 tbsp apple cider vinegar (for a better rise and texture)
- 1 ¼ cups almond flour (finely ground for best surface)
- ¼ cup coconut flour (adds structure and a light surface)
- ¼ cup ground flaxseed (for fiber and surface)
- ¼ cup psyllium husk powder (essential for restricting and surface in low-carb breads)
- 2 tbsp erythritol or another low-carb sugar (optional, to adjust flavors)
- 1 tsp salt
- 1 tbsp baking powder

- 1 tsp dynamic dry yeast or instant yeast (optional, for flavor as opposed to rise)

Guidelines

1. Set up the Bread Machine

Set your bread machine to the gluten-free or low-carb setting if available. In the event that nor is accessible, utilize the quick bread or cake setting as this bread doesn't have to rise in the conventional manner.

2. Add Wet Fixings

Pour the warm water, olive oil, eggs, and apple cider vinegar into the bread machine pan.

3. Add Dry Fixings

Add the almond flour, coconut flour, ground flaxseed, psyllium husk powder, erythritol (if using), salt, baking powder, and yeast on top of the wet fixings.

4. Start the Bread Machine

Select the gluten-free or speedy bread setting and begin the machine. This bread won't rise much because of the low-carb flours, so a shorter baking time is great.

5.   Check Consistency

Following 5-10 minutes of mixing, take a look at the
mixture's consistency. It ought to be thick and marginally
sticky, similar to a biscuit player. If excessively thick, add a
tablespoon of water at a time until it reaches the right
consistency.

6.   Bake and Cool

Allow the bread machine to finish its baking cycle. The
bread ought to come out golden brown with a firm crust.

7.   Cool Totally

Remove the bread from the pan and let it cool on a wire
rack. Cooling totally helps the bread set and makes it
simpler to slice.

8.   Cut and Enjoy

Once cooled, cut and enjoy your low-carb, gluten-free bread
as a sandwich base, toast, or a low-carb snack.

Paleo-Friendly gluten-free Bread

This Paleo-friendly gluten-free Bread is a good and nutritious portion that fits impeccably into a gluten-free grain and dairy-free diet. Made with almond flour, coconut flour, and a mix of healthy fats, it is soft, slightly thick, and flexible enough for toast, sandwiches, or a side to your favorite Paleo meal. The recipe is basic, depending on natural, Whole-food fixings, making it ideal for those following a Paleo lifestyle.

Fixings

- ¾ cup warm water (around 110°F or 43°C)
- ¼ cup olive oil or dissolved coconut oil
- 3 huge eggs (room temperature)
- 1 tbsp apple cider vinegar (assists with surface and rise)
- 1 ½ cups almond flour (finely ground for best surface)
- ¼ cup coconut flour (adds structure and dampness)
- ¼ cup ground flaxseed (for surface and restricting)
- 2 tbsp custard starch (optional, for a slightly chewier surface)

- 1 tbsp honey (optional, to add an inconspicuous pleasantness)
- 1 tsp salt
- 1 tbsp baking powder
- 1 tsp dynamic dry yeast (optional, for flavor instead of rise)

Directions

1. Set up the Bread Machine

Set your bread machine to the gluten-free setting if accessible. if x not, utilize the fast bread or cake setting, as this bread doesn't have to rise.

2. Add Wet Fixings

Pour the warm water, olive oil, eggs, apple cider vinegar, and honey (if using) into the bread machine pan.

3. Add Dry Fixings

On top of the wet fixings, add the almond flour, coconut flour, ground flaxseed, custard starch (if using), salt, baking powder, and yeast (if using) to the pan.

4. Start the Bread Machine

Select the gluten-free or quick bread setting and turn on the machine.

5. Check Consistency

Following 5-10 minutes of blending, really take a look at the mixture's consistency. It would be ideal for it to be thick and sticky, like muffin batter. If it's excessively thick, add a tablespoon of water at a time until it arrives at the right consistency. if excessively wet, add a little more coconut flour.

6. Bake and Cool

Permit the bread machine to finish its baking cycle. The bread ought to emerge with a brilliant outside and a firm top.

7. Cool Totally

Remove the bread from the skillet and let it cool on a wire rack prior to cutting. Cooling completely will help the bread set and make slicing easier

8. Cut and Enjoy

Once cooled, cut and enjoy your Paleo-friendly bread with your favorite toppings.

Grain-free keto Bread

This grain-free Keto Bread is a low-carb, gluten-free portion ideal for those following a ketogenic or grain-free diet. Made with almond flour, eggs, and solid fats, this bread is thick, delightful, and an incredible substitute for conventional high-carb portions. Whether you use it for sandwiches, toast, or as a dessert, this keto-friendly bread fits well into a low-carb lifestyle while still giving the fulfillment of natively constructed bread.

Fixings

- 1 cup warm water (around 110°F or 43°C)
- ¼ cup olive oil or softened coconut oil
- 3 huge eggs (room temperature)
- 1 tbsp apple cider vinegar (assists with rise and surface)
- 1 ½ cups almond flour (finely ground for best surface)
- ¼ cup coconut flour (adds structure and decreases moisture)
- ¼ cup psyllium husk powder (significant for structure and restricting)
- 2 tbsp ground flaxseed (optional, for extra surface)

- **1 tbsp baking powder**
- 1 tsp salt
- 1 tsp dynamic dry yeast (optional, for flavor only cause it won't raise the bread)

Directions

1. Set up the Bread Machine

Set your bread machine to the gluten-free or low-carb setting if available. If not, utilize the fast bread or cake setting, as this bread doesn't need a conventional rise.

2. Add Wet Fixings

Pour the warm water, olive oil, eggs, and apple cider vinegar into the bread machine pan.

3. Add Dry Fixings

Add the almond flour, coconut flour, psyllium husk powder, ground flaxseed (if using), baking powder, salt, and yeast on top of the wet fixings. The yeast will add flavor but won't affect the rise as in conventional bread.

4. Begin the Bread Machine

Select the without gluten or fast bread setting and begin the machine.

5. Check Consistency

After around 5-10 minutes of mixing, take a look at the mixture's consistency. It would be ideal for it to be thick and sticky, looking like a thick batter. If it's excessively thick, add 1 tablespoon of water at a time. If excessively wet, add a little more coconut flour.

6. Bake and Cool

Allow the bread machine to finish its baking cycle. The portion ought to come out with a golden crust and firm surface.

7. Cool Totally

Remove the bread from the machine dish and let it cool on a wire rack. This will assist it to firm up and make cutting simpler.

8. Cut and Enjoy

Once cooled, cut your grain-free keto bread and enjoy it as a low-carb alternative for sandwiches, toast, or as a nibble with your favorite toppings.

Allergen-free (nut-free, dairy free, and egg free) gluten-free Bread

This allergen-free Bread is intended to address the issues of those staying away from normal allergens like nuts, dairy, and eggs, while as yet being altogether gluten-free. Made with basic, healthy fixings, this bread is ideally suited for anybody with different dietary limitations, offering a soft, somewhat chewy surface that is great for sandwiches, toast, or just enjoying it alone. It's an amazing choice for families and people with food awareness or sensitivities.

Fixings

- 1 ½ cups warm water (around 110°F or 43°C)
- ¼ cup olive oil or vegetable oil
- 2 tbsp maple syrup or agave syrup (optional, for a dash of softness)
- 1 tbsp apple cider vinegar (further develops rise and surface)
- 2 ½ cups gluten-free regular flour mix (guarantee it incorporates xanthan or guar gum; if not, add 1 tsp thickener)

- ½ cup custard starch or potato starch (adds softness and chew)
- 1 tbsp ground flaxseed (optional, adds surface)
- 1 ½ tsp salt
- 1 tbsp baking powder
- 2 tsp dynamic dry yeast or active yeast (guarantee it's gluten-free)

Directions

1. Set up the Bread Machine

Set your bread machine to the gluten-free setting if available. if not, utilize the essential or fast back setting, as this bread doesn't need a conventional rise.

2. Add Wet Fixings

Add the warm water, olive oil, maple syrup (if using), and apple cider vinegar to the bread machine pan.

3. Add Dry Fixings

Add the gluten-free flour mix, custard starch, ground flaxseed, salt, and baking powder on top of the wet fixings.

4. Add Yeast

Make a little well in the middle of the dry fixings and add the yeast. This helps keep the yeast dry until blending starts

5. Start the Bread Machine

Select the gluten-free or basis setting and start the machine.

6. Check Mixture Consistency

After around 5-10 minutes of blending,Take a look at the batter's consistency. It ought to be thick and somewhat sticky yet properly mixed. If its excessively dry, add more warm water, 1 tablespoon at a time. If it's excessively wet, add more gluten-free flour.

7. Bake and Cool

Allow the bread machine to finish its baking cycle. The bread ought to emerge with a brilliant brown crust and a soft inside.

8. Cool Totally

Cautiously remove the bread from the machine and let it cool on a wire rack. Cooling completely prior to cutting will help improve the surface.

9. Cut and Enjoy

Once cooled, cut your allergen-free bread and enjoy it with spreads, sandwiches, or all alone!

Troubleshooting and FAQs

Indeed, even the most experienced gluten-free cooks can run into issues while making bread. In this chapter we would discuss some common issues and frequently asked questions to help you investigate and perfect your gluten-free bread machine recipes.

Common Issues and Handy solutions

Baking gluten-free bread can some of the time present difficulties, particularly in the event that you're unfamiliar with it. Here is a rundown of normal issues you could experience and handy solutions to assist you with accomplishing an effective loaf like clockwork.

1. Bread is Excessively Thick

- Issue: The bread feels weighty and doesn't rise as expected.

Convenient solution:

- Ensure your yeast is new and dynamic (active). In the case of utilizing dry yeast, proof it in warm water with a touch of sugar prior to adding it to the blend.

- Increase how much raising agents (baking powder or baking soda) slightly.

- Incorporate a light, vaporous flour, similar to custard or potato starch, to ease up the surface.

2. Bread Falls in the Center

Issue: The portion rises well yet sinks once it cools.

Convenient solution:

- Reduce how much fluid is in the recipe.

- Avoid over proofing the batter; screen the rise intently and bake when it has generally multiplied in size.

- Use a blend of flours that give better structural integrity, for example, utilizing psyllium husk.

3. Bread is Sticky Inside

Issue: The inside is wet and sticky.

Handy solution:

- Bake the bread longer. Gluten-free bread frequently demands extra time contrasted with conventional bread.

- Check the temperature inside the loaf with a thermometer; it ought to reach around 200°F (93°C) when completely heated.
- Allow the bread to cool totally in the dish prior to cutting to guarantee legitimate surface.

4. Bread is Excessively Brittle

Issue: The cuts falls apart easily.

Handy solution:

- Ensure you're using an adequate number of restricting agents, similar to eggs, flaxseed meal, or chia seeds.
- Add moisture by integrating extra fluid fixings, similar to fruit purée or yogurt, to the recipe.
- Check your flour mix; some may not give sufficient surface.

5. Bread Doesn't Rise

Issue: The mixture stays flat and doesn't rise enough.

Handy solution:

- Ensure the yeast is dynamic; confirmation it as referenced before.
- Increase the temperature during rising, as gluten-free bread benefits from a slightly hotter setting.
- Consider adding more yeast.

6. Bread Has an Off Taste or Smell

Issue: The bread tastes bizarre or smell funny.

Handy solution:

- Check the newness of your fixings, particularly the flour and baking soda/baking powder.
- If utilizing almond flour, guarantee it's not smelly; it has a shorter timeframe of natural usability than different flours.
- Balance flavors by adding spices, flavors, or a bit of sweeteners (like honey or maple syrup) to cover any unpleasant taste.

7. Bread Sinks In after Baking

Issue: The portion shows up fine while baking however implodes once out of the bread machine.

Handy solution:

- Reduce how much yeast or allow the mixture to rise less prior to baking.
- Monitor the baking time intently; guarantee it's completely cooked prior to removing it from the machine.
- Avoid unexpected changes in temperature by allowing the bread to cool slowly.

8. Crust is Excessively Hard

Issue: The covering turns out tough or excessively thick.

Convenient solution:

- Cover the portion with foil part of the way through baking to relax the outside.
- Brush the highest point of the loaf with oil or liquefied margarine prior to baking for a milder crust.
- Experiment with adding more water to the mixture.

to make delightful portions By understanding these normal issues and their handy solutions, you can troubleshoot successfully and enjoy the time spent baking gluten-free bread. With training, you'll track down the ideal harmony between fixings and strategies that meet your dietary necessities!

The most effective method to Adjust Recipes to Your Bread Machine

Adjusting gluten-free bread recipes to your bread machine can be a pleasant and exciting process. While most recipes can be adapted to machine use, it's fundamental to consider the interesting attributes of gluten-free fixings and the particular elements of your bread machine. This is the way to effectively adjust recipes to obtain the best outcomes:

1. Comprehend Your Bread Machine

• Know the Settings: Find out more about your machine's settings, especially the gluten-free setting, if available. This setting ordinarily changes the working and rising times to suit gluten-free batter, which acts uniquely in contrast to conventional wheat mixture.

• Limit Matters: Ensure the recipe accommodates your machine's ability. Most machines can deal with 1.5 to 2-pound portions. If a recipe yields a bigger portion, change the fixing amounts relatively.

2. Pick the Right Recipe

• Select gluten-free Recipes: Begin with recipes explicitly intended for sans gluten baking. These recipes represent the absence of gluten and incorporate appropriate fixings to assist with accomplishing the ideal surface and rise.

• Search for high rise Recipes: Select recipes that yield lighter portions. Fixings like psyllium husk or thickener can assist with copying the structure gluten gives.

3. Change Fixings

• Flour Mixes: Use a gluten-free regular flour mix that incorporates thickener or psyllium husk for better surface. In the event that your mix does exclude folios, consider adding 1 teaspoon of thickener to your flour.

• Fluid Proportions: sans gluten flours will quite often ingest more fluid. Begin by adding more fluid than the recipe calls for and change depending on the situation to accomplish a thick however pourable batter.

• Add Fasteners: Incorporate folios like flaxseed meal or chia seeds, which can upgrade the surface and moisture content.

4. Adjust Blending and Rising Times

• More shorter Blending Time: gluten-free mixture doesn't need a similar degree of blending as wheat-based batter. Blend just until the fixings are joined and a batter forms.

• Rising Changes: gluten-free batter normally demands less rising investment. Screen the batter intently; it ought to rise until it's about twofold in size yet stay away from over proofing.

5. Try different things with Temperature

• Warm Fixings: Utilize warm fluids (not hot) to assist with activating the yeast. This can likewise assist the mixture with rising all the more successfully.

• Warm Rising Climate: In the event that your kitchen is cold, consider establishing a warm climate for ascending by setting the bread machine in a warm region or turning on the stove briefly and putting the machine close by.

6. Screen Baking Times

• Check Doneness Early: gluten-free bread might prepare quicker or more slow than customary bread. Begin checking for doneness a couple of moments before the finish of the recommended baking time.

• Utilize a Thermometer: The inner temperature of sans gluten bread ought to reach around 200°F (93°C) for it to be completely cooked.

7. Trial and Record

• Take Notes: Each bread machine and recipe might require slight changes. Keep notes on what works and what doesn't, including fixing proportions, blending times, and baking spans.

• Experimentation: Be encouraged by starting disappointments. Gluten-free baking frequently requires a trial and error to perfect recipes for your particular machine.

8. Storing left over

• Proper storage: In the wake of baking, let the bread cool totally prior to putting it away. Utilize a hermetically sealed compartment at room temperature or freeze slice for future use.

• Refresh Prior to Serving: Assuming the bread becomes old, you can refresh it by toasting cuts.

Freezing and Storing gluten-free Bread

Appropriately putting away gluten-free bread is fundamental to keeping up with its newness and surface. Gluten-free bread will in general have a shorter timeframe of realistic usability than conventional bread due to absence of preservatives and gluten, which holds moisture. Here are a few powerful strategies for freezing and storing gluten-free bread:

1. Cooling Prior to Storing

• Allow it to cool totally: After baking, allow the bread to cool totally on a wire rack. This keeps condensation from forming, which can prompt sogginess and mold.

• Abstain from Cutting Too early: Hold on until the bread has cooled totally before to cutting. Cutting too soon can lead to uneven surface and increase the rise of a sticky inside.

2. Short-term Storage

• Room Temperature: For short-term storage (as long as 2 days), keep gluten-free bread in a water/air proof container or a re-sealable plastic pack at room temperature. This helps maintain moisture without catching excess humidity.

• Paper Towel trick: To keep the crust soft, you can enclose the bread with a paper towel prior to putting it in a pack container.

3. Freezing for Long-term Storage

• Cut Prior to Freezing: Assuming you intend to freeze your bread, think about cutting it ahead of time. This permits you to take out just the cuts you really want, guaranteeing you don't need to defrost the whole portion each time.

• Wrap Appropriately: Wrap the bread firmly in plastic wrap or aluminum foil, then, at that point, place it in a cooler safe re-sealable sack. Remove as much air as could possible to avoid freezer burn.

• Mark and Date: Name the pack with the date and kind of bread to monitor how long it has been in the cooler.

4. Defrosting gluten-free Bread

• Countertop method: For the best texture, defrost frozen cuts at room temperature. This normally requires around 15-30 minutes, depending on the thickness of the cuts.

• Toaster Method: You can toast cuts directly from freezer for a fast and simple choice. This strategy improves the surface and flavor while giving a warm, firm completion.

• Oven Method: If you have an entire portion, you can defrost it in the broiler. Preheat the oven to 350°F (175°C), enclose the portion by aluminum foil, and intensity for around 20-30 minutes or until defrosted.

5. Refrigeration Contemplations

• Stay away from Refrigeration: Generally, it's ideal to try not to store gluten-free bread in the fridge. The chilly temperature can dry out the bread and lead to a stale surface. In the event that you should refrigerate, do so just for brief periods and guarantee it's in an air-tight container.

6. Refreshing left over Bread

• Restoring Stale Bread: If your gluten-free bread has become flat, you can revive it by gently sprinkling water on the outside layer and warming it in the stove for around 5-10 minutes at 350°F (175°C). This reestablishes some moisture and improve surface.

Ways to warm gluten-free Bread

Warming gluten-free bread can be an incredible method for reestablishing its freshness and work on its surface. Here are a few compelling ways to warm various sorts of gluten-free bread:

1. Toaster Technique

• Toast Frozen: if you have frozen gluten-free bread, you can toast cuts directly from the cooler. Set your toaster to a medium setting and toast until golden brown.

• Avoid Over-toasting: Watch out for the bread to avoid burning, as gluten-free bread can toast more rapidly than customary bread.

2. Microwave Technique

• Short Burst: place a piece of gluten-free bread on a microwave-safe plate and cover it with a clammy paper towel. Heat in short time frames 15 seconds. Take a look after every interval to keep it from becoming tough or rubbery.

• Limit Microwave Use: Microwaving is helpful however can prompt a chewy surface. Utilize this strategy for speedy warming when you're in a rush.

3. Skillet Technique

• Heat a Skillet: Preheat a non-stick skillet over medium intensity. You can softly grease the skillet with spread or oil for added character.

• Toast the two Sides: Place a piece of bread in the skillet and toast for around 2-3 minutes on each side until warmed through and marginally fresh. This strategy gives a pleasant mash to the outside.

4. Barbecue or Panini Press

• Utilize a Barbecue or Press: For a delectably fresh outside, you can utilize a barbecue dish or a panini press. Preheat the press, place the bread inside, and close it for a couple of seconds until warmed.

• Add Fixings: This technique is likewise perfect if you need to make barbecued cheddar or other sandwiches, adding cheddar or different fillings for additional flavor.

5. Reviving stale Bread

• Sprinkle Water: if the bread is stale, you can sprinkle a couple of drops of water on the outside prior to warming. This restores moisture during the warming process.

• Cover with a Towel: On the other hand, cover the bread with a moist material while warming in the stove or microwave to trap steam and further improve.

6. Be Time Conscious

• Avoid Overheating: sans gluten bread can become dry whenever warmed for a really long time. Continuously check for warmth and texture to guarantee it doesn't lose its quality.

By following these ways to warm gluten-free bread, you can appreciate warm, crisp tasting cuts that keep up with their superb surface. Whether you're warming cuts or entire portions, these techniques will assist you with relishing your gluten-free bread to its fullest!

Conclusion

Baking gluten-free bread can be a superb culinary experience, exploring a world of textures and flavors custom-made to your dietary necessities. With the right methods and information, you can make tasty portions that rival conventional bread. By understanding how to adjust recipes to your bread machine, appropriately store and freeze your manifestations, and successfully warm them, you'll guarantee that your gluten-free bread stays fresh and charming. Embrace the cycle, try different things with various fixings, and before long you'll wind up excelling at gluten-free baking, one loaf at a time!

Your gluten-free Baking Journey

Setting out on a gluten-free baking journey isn't just about following recipes; it's a thrilling investigation of flavors, surfaces, and inventiveness. Whether you're new to gluten-free baking or hoping to refine your abilities, here are a bits of knowledge and support to direct you through this amazing experience.

1. Embrace the Expectation to learn and adapt

Progressing at gluten-free baking might require a few changes and trial and error. Gluten-free flours and fixings act differently in contrast to their gluten-containing partners, and you could experience difficulties along the way. Embrace these opportunity as an open door to learn and develop. Keep notes on what works and what doesn't, and hesitate to make changes as needed.

2. Investigate Various Ingredients

Gluten-free baking makes the way to explore different kinds of flours and binders. From almond and coconut flour to rice flour and custard starch, every fixing brings its unique flavor and surface. Trying different things with various blends can prompt brilliant revelations, whether you're making an classic portion, an savory bread, or a sweet treat.

3. Get Innovative with Recipes

When you feel alright with the basics, don't hesitate to be creative Adjust customary recipes by subbing gluten-free fixings, adding flavors, spices, or try experimenting with flavors like chocolate or fruits. Your gluten-free baking journey is a potential chance to put your own twist on adored recipes.

4. Engage with a community

Connecting with other people who share your gluten-free baking energy can unimaginably remunerate. Join online forums, virtual entertainment gatherings, or nearby baking classes where you can trade tips, share triumphs, and look for counsel. Connecting with fellow bakers can motivate you and provide support.

5. Observe Your Accomplishments

Each loaf you bake is a step in the right direction in your gluten-free baking excursion. Praise your victories, whether it's accomplishing the ideal rise, mastering another recipe, or essentially enjoying a warm cut of bread straight from the broiler. Acknowledging your improvement and invest wholeheartedly in the delightful manifestations you produce.

6. Maintain an open mind

Gluten-free baking is a constantly developing craftsmanship. Remain open to new methods, fixings, and thoughts. As you gain certainty, you might end up needing to try further, making your special recipes that mirror your preferences and dietary necessities.

7. Enjoy the process

Most importantly, recollect that baking ought to be enjoyable! Take some time to relish the cycle, from mixing fixings to the awesome fragrance floating through your kitchen. Each baking session is a potential chance to learn, investigate, and make something delightful.

Testing and Modifying Recipes

Baking gluten-free bread can be a fulfilling and inventive undertaking, permitting you to fit recipes to your own inclinations and dietary requirements. Testing and redoing recipes is critical to finding one of a kind flavors and surfaces that suit your sense of taste. Here are a few hints and rules to assist you with exploring this interesting part of gluten-free baking:

1. Grasp the Fundamentals

• Know Your Fixings: Find out more about the various sorts of gluten-free flours (e.g., almond, coconut, Brown colored rice) and their properties. Each flour has unmistakable qualities that influence flavor, surface, and moisture content.

• Restricting Specialists: Comprehend the job of restricting specialists like thickener, psyllium husk, and flaxseed meal, which assist with emulating the design and flexibility that gluten gives in conventional bread.

2. Begin with a Base Recipe

• Pick a Solid Recipe: Start with a gluten-free bread recipe that has great surveys and demonstrated results. This will give you a strong groundwork to work from.

• Dissect the Fixings: Separate the recipe to figure out the extents and elements of every ingredients. Knowing how they collaborate will assist you with making informed replacements.

3. Roll out Gradual Improvements

• Replacement Technique: While tweaking, roll out each improvement in turn. For instance, to utilize almond flour rather than a gluten-free generally useful mix, Try it in a little group first to check the outcomes.

• Change Proportions: gluten-free flours frequently require different fluid proportions. Assuming you're subbing flours, be ready to change the fluid in the recipe to accomplish the right consistency.

4. Integrate Flavors and Add-Ins

• Flavor Upgrades: Experimenting with adding flavors, spices, or flavor extricates (like vanilla or almond) to your mixture for an extraordinary turn. Fixings like garlic powder, rosemary, or cinnamon can raise your bread.

• Blend In's: Add seeds, nuts, dried natural products, or chocolate chips to make customized variants of your bread. Simply be aware of what these augmentations might mean for dampness and surface.

5. Play with sweeteners

• Sweet versus savory: Modify the sweetness of your bread based on your preference. Remove sugar for a less sweet portion or add honey, maple syrup, or fruit puree for natural sweetness.

• Alternative Sugars: Investigate using alternative sugars like stevia, agave, or coconut sugar, remembering that they might change the moisture levels in your batter.

6. Experiment different Surface

• Softness and crust: if you favor a gentler crust, consider adding yogurt, fruit purée, or oil to the recipe. For a crispier outside, increase the baking time or prepare at a higher temperature.

• Rise and Thickness: Changing how much yeast or using baking powder can assist with controlling the rise and thickness of your bread. Explore different avenues regarding both to track down your favored texture.

7. Record Your Examinations

• Keep a Baking Diary: Record your fixing changes, estimations, baking times, and results in a baking diary. This documentation will assist you with refining your recipes and recreate victories.

• Take Notes on Flavors and Surfaces: Note what various fixings mean for the flavor and texture of your bread. This will help you in making future changes.

8. Embrace Slip-ups

• Gaining from Disappointments: Few out of every odd analysis will yield the ideal outcomes, and that is entirely alright! Use disappointments for learning amazing chances to comprehend what turned out badly and how to work on something better.

• Remain Positive: Embrace the inventive approach, and recollect that each endeavor carries you nearer to dominating your gluten-free baking abilities.

9. Offer and Gather Feedback

• Taste Testing: Offer your creations with loved ones. Their input can give important experiences and rouse groundbreaking thoughts for your next baking sessions.

• Engage with community: Associate with other gluten-free bakers on the web or in person to trade thoughts, tips, and recipe variations.

Testing and redoing recipes is at the core of gluten-free baking, permitting you to find new flavors and surfaces that suit your taste. By figuring out the nuts and bolts, rolling out slow improvements, and archiving your journey, you can make heavenly gluten-free breads that mirror your novel style. Enjoy all the process and happy baking!

Made in United States
Orlando, FL
21 December 2024

56292002R00075